The Isles of
SCILLY

Gathering seaweed from the rocks for burning, *c.*1875

The Isles of
SCILLY

Luke Over

with illustrations from
The Gibson Collection

Phillimore

1993

Published by
PHILLIMORE & CO. LTD.,
Shopwyke Manor Barn, Chichester, Sussex

ISBN 0 85033 884 0

Printed and bound in Great Britain by
BIDDLES LTD.,
Guildford, Surrey

This book is dedicated to my wife Maureen,
who for 25 years has endured interrupted beach holidays
because of my historical studies in the Isles of Scilly

Contents

List of Illustrations

Frontispiece: Gathering seaweed from the rocks for burning.

ix

Acknowledgements

In the production of this book I should like to record my thanks to Mr. Frank Gibson for allowing me to use photographs from the famous Gibson Collection. Five members of the family, with more than 250 active years work between them have photographed the islands for more than a century.

Thanks are due to the Gibson Collection for the following illustrations: frontispiece, 1, 2, 13, 14, 18, 19, 25, 27, 29, 38, 39, 44, 46, 47, 50-52, 54, 64, 66-79, 82-89, 93, 95, 96, 99, 102-116, 119-128, 131-136, 138-140, 142, 144, 146, 148, 150.

All other photographs are from the author's collection.

In general I should like to thank the people of Scilly, who have always been friendly and helpful to me over the last 25 years, and those bodies who work diligently to preserve the environment for generations to come.

Finally, my thanks to Veronica Kempton for typing the manuscript.

1.   A winter storm on Porthcressa Beach.

Chapter 1

Submergence and Settlement

The Isles of Scilly lie some 28 miles west of Land's End in the Atlantic Ocean. The archipelago today comprises some two hundred islands and rocks, of which only a dozen can be considered to be of any size and only five are inhabited. The main island, measuring 2½ miles across, is St Mary's which is joined to the Hugh or Garrison Island by a sand bar on which the principal settlement of Hugh Town is situated. Visitors travelling from the mainland in the majority of cases will arrive by boat or helicopter from Penzance to St Mary's or at the heliport situated there.

Boats leave St Mary's daily for the inhabited off-islands of Tresco, Bryher, St Martin's and St Agnes. Tresco is perhaps the best known for its sub-tropical gardens planted in the early 19th century, and faces the island of Bryher. St Martin's is the most northerly and is joined to White Island at low tide, whilst St Agnes is linked to the uninhabited isle of Gugh by a sand bar, which is occasionally covered at high tide.

Of the uninhabited islands Samson is the largest and was once populated in the 19th century. The smaller islands of St Helen's and Tean, to the west

2.   Seasickness affects Victorians en route to Scilly.

1

3. An early map of the Isles of Scilly prepared for Henry, Duke of Grafton.

TO HIS ROYAL HIGHNESS
WILLIAM DUKE OF CUMBERLAND,
CAPTAIN GENERAL OF ALL HIS
MAJESTY'S FORCES &c.
This Plate is most humbly
dedicated, by His Royal Highness's
most dutiful & most obedient Servant
Robert Heath

Scale of Two Miles.

Published according to Act of Parliament by R. Manby & H.S. Cox Booksellers, on Ludgate

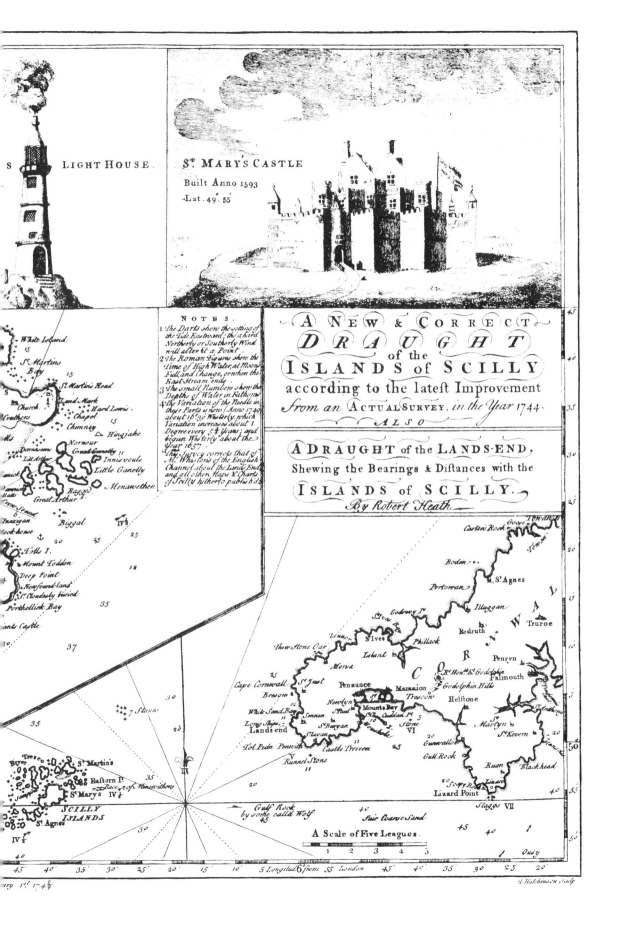

4. Early attempts at tin mining on Castle Down, Tresco.

of St Martin's were also populated in antiquity but are now the haunt of nesting birds. The nearby Round Island supports a lighthouse to guide shipping passing to the north of the archipelago. The island of Annet to the west of St Agnes houses colonies of puffins, manx shearwaters and storm petrels and is closed to the visitor during the nesting season.

There are three groups of smaller isles which merit mentioning. The Northern Isles are situated to the west of Bryher and comprise mainly large rocks of which Scilly Rock, after which some say the archipelago was named, is one. The Eastern Isles are slightly larger land masses worthy of exploration, and include Great and Little Arthur, Great and Little Ganilly and Nornour. The Western Rocks, which are situated around the Bishop Rock Lighthouse, are the last pieces of land before America and support a large seal population.

Scilly is touched by the Gulf Stream and therefore the climate tends to be mild all year round although the islands are regularly affected during the winter by south westerly gales. Frost and snow are rare, enabling sub-tropical plants to flourish, and daffodils to bloom early for the Covent Garden market. The atmosphere is entirely unpolluted and sunlight very strong, which is a great attraction to the visitor, as is the translucent blue sea which is due to the lack of plankton and microscopic organisms in the water. These features, together with the numerous white sandy beaches which surround all the islands, bring large numbers of tourists on an annual pilgrimage to Scilly, thus helping to boost the Islands' economy.

The original rock of the islands was a grey slatey material known as killas which was laid down more than 600 million years ago, and a patch of this can still be found on the north west side of White Island off St Martin's. Other than this, the islands that we see today are part of a line of granite bosses which start on Dartmoor and descend through Devon and Cornwall to Scilly.

In theory this granite should contain tin, but not apparently in any quantity. There are a few historical records of tin being found from open cast mining, but an example of this can be seen on Tresco. However, unless large quantities were removed in antiquity, the islands have never been particularly rich in supplies of this metal.

During the last million years the land mass of Scilly was subject to the extreme climatic changes of the Ice Ages. During the glacial phases the ice cap at the North Pole was extended and the sea level dropped, while the inter-glacial phases had the reverse effect. These variations in sea level brought about the formation of beaches at the corresponding levels and raised beaches can be detected on the northern fringes of Tresco, Bryher and St Martin's at a height of 40 feet above the present sea level. Carn Leh, a fossil stack in Old Town Bay, St Mary's, records three ancient shorelines at heights of 25, 44 and 64 feet.

There is considerable evidence to show that when the islands were first inhabited, and certainly by 3000 B.C., they were twice the size that they are now. The water between the islands is very

5. Carn Leh, Old Town, St Mary's, a fossil stack which records the heights of three previous sea levels.

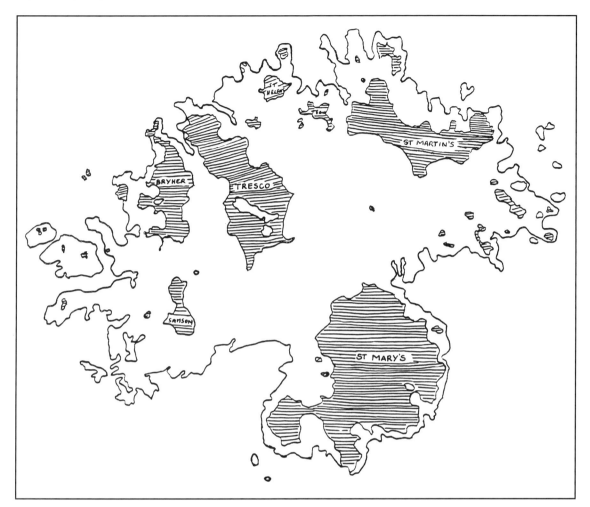

6. A line drawn around the 25-ft. marine contour, showing the possible original shape of Scilly when it was one land mass.

7. The Nag's Head, St Agnes, a natural granite formation.

shallow, and if a line is drawn around the 25-foot contour, some indication of the earlier shape can be ascertained. It would appear that the islands of St Mary's, Bryher, Tresco and St Martin's together with the Eastern Isles formed one large land mass, which has been subject to steady erosion by the sea as its level rose. In the form they are today the islands represent the higher elevations of the former single island. St Agnes and Gugh probably formed a second island, with Annet and the Western Rocks as two smaller land masses.

Present evidence suggests that the formation of modern day Scilly was not complete until the 16th century and even in the 11th century most islands would have been joined at low water. This evidence comes from the fact that early Cornish placenames are found around the outer edges of the islands, whilst inward facing shores, which were formed after the breaking up of the main island, were given English names some time after 1600. Whilst exact details of the submergence are not entirely clear, its occurrence is indicated by the many prehistoric, Roman and later sites which are now below water level. These include houses, graves and field walls which indicate settlements and low-lying arable ground which was lost through marine inundation. Examples of these can be seen during spring tides on Samson Flats, Appletree Bay, Tresco, and Green Bay, Bryher. Divers have also noticed walls beneath the water at Little Arthur and other parts of the Eastern Isles.

Today, Scilly is very much a treeless landscape with the exception of those deliberately as wind-breaks planted during the 19th century. However, peat samples taken from the Higher and Lower Moors on St Mary's show that during the 6th millennium B.C. the Islands were covered by oak woodland, with patches of elm and ash. Around 1500 B.C. there was a marked decline in wood-land, and flora samples indicate a more open and pastoral landscape suitable for the cultivation of crops. This clearance probably equates to the arrival of the first settlers to the islands.

There is no substantial evidence for settlement in the island prior to the early Bronze Age in 2500 B.C. There are one or two early implements on display in the museum which, on the face of it, appear to belong to the Neolithic period of the third millennium B.C. These comprise one end scraper, part of a macehead and a polished stone axe from Gugh. A further stone axe from Gugh is known to have been found in addition to another found on St Mary's. These artifacts alone cannot be considered as evidence of habitation and so far no dwellings or tombs of the Neolithic culture have been discovered. However, it is possible that land subsidence has destroyed all traces of occupation and the evidence has vanished beneath the sea.

8.   Appletree Bay, Tresco. Field walls and stone remains revealed on a spring tide. The island of Samson can be seen in the background.

9. A well-preserved entrance tomb at Innisidgen, St Mary's.

10. One of the many Bronze Age chambered tombs on Kittern Hill, Gugh.

11. Bants Carn burial mound, St Mary's, showing stone revetments.

12. A Bronze Age cist burial on North Hill, Samson.

The first settlers, of whom we have considerable evidence, arrived in Scilly around 2000 B.C. Their origins lay in Southern Spain and Portugal where, at an earlier date, there was a flourishing copper-using civilisation. This maritime culture spread to Brittany, Cornwall and the western and northern parts of Britain and their route is clearly marked by a series of megalithic tombs which occur in all these areas, although there are regional variations.

The Isles of Scilly can boast at least 150 burial mounds or barrows from the Bronze Age, and no less than 45 of these are of megalithic type and contain stone burial chambers. Two of these are classed as Passage Graves and the others as Entrance Graves. In the whole of Cornwall there are only 17 known Entrance Graves and this infers that Scilly was a favoured spot for these particular tomb builders. So large is the proportion of tombs that classical writers have referred to Scilly as the 'Isles of the Dead' and it has been suggested that inhabitants from the mainland were conveyed there after death for burial. This is not the case, however, as traces of dwellings have been found on the water's edge and undoubtedly whole villages of huts have disappeared beneath the sea. What now remains of the land in Scilly represents the higher elevations of what was a much larger land mass, and it was not unusual for prehistoric man to erect tombs on hilltops.

The barrows of Scilly are circular and have an average diameter of 30 feet, although some examples are up to sixty feet across. They are composed of stones and earth and the consistency varies from nearly all earth to nearly all stones. In other parts of Britain barrows made entirely of stone are known as cairns or carns. However, in Scilly the word 'carn' is used to denote a natural outcrop of rock, and visitors should bear this in mind when reading maps of the islands.

It was the practice of the Bronze Age people to place a burial by inhumation or cremation in the centre of the mound, and the unchambered barrows of Scilly would have contained one burial only at, or just below, the original ground level. Where little stone was used in the building of the barrow, constant erosion by the elements over the last 4,000 years will have reduced the mound to ground level, leaving little trace of its existence. Where, however, a revetment of stones was used to hold the earthen mound in place, these may still remain as a clue to the location of a barrow.

By far the most impressive and substantial tombs in Scilly are those which contain stone burial chambers. These were designed as family or communal vaults and received the remains of large numbers of people over a period of several hundred years. The chambers vary in size and are generally smaller than tombs on the mainland. The side and back walls are composed either of large upright stones or smaller stones held together by a crude form of mortar and the roofs are made of massive capstones designed to support the weight of the earth placed on the chamber. The entrance to the chamber is at ground level and two examples at Porthellick and Bants Carn on St Mary's have passages leading to the chamber and as such are termed as passage graves.

A majority of these tombs have been long since rifled of their contents by treasure hunters, thus robbing the archaeologists of valuable information. Excavations have been carried out, however, and enough evidence obtained to piece together their history. The earliest known work was by Dr. Borlase in the mid-18th century, who, having hired some soldiers, dug into some barrows on St Mary's. Even at this time it would appear that the tombs had been robbed as he reported that 'we discovered nothing but the structure of them neither could I find, upon the strictest enquiry, that even any

13.   John and Alexander Gibson, Scilly photographers, at Piper's Hole, a natural formation on Tresco.

urn was found in Scilly'. Further more he observed that the inhabitants considered the mounds to be the tombs of giants and hesitated to interfere with them lest they should incur the wrath of the same. As it was, the night after Dr. Borlase had excavated, a violent storm struck Scilly and ruined the crops of the inhabitants, who blamed him for disturbing the peace of the giants. He could not persuade them otherwise which is not surprising as superstitions die hard when backed up with actual happenings like this.

At the turn of the century further work was carried out by George Bonsor, a British subject residing in Spain. During the years 1899-1901 he investigated burial chambers on St Mary's, Gugh and Samson and carried out what can be considered the first scientific excavation in Scilly, that of Obadiah's barrow on Gugh. The evidence showed that the chamber had been in use over a long period and that the first burials had been inhumations, followed later in the Bronze Age by a series of cremations, traces of which at least a dozen were found. Whilst investigating other chambers on Kittern Hill, Gugh, he noticed that there were ten mounds in the vicinity, containing charcoal and blackened sand. These, he considered, may have been the places where the cremations took place.

A more up-to-date excavation using the latest techniques took place in 1948, and was conducted by B. H. St J. O'Neill for the Department of the Environment. This was at Knackyboy Cairn, St Martin's, where the contents of a large part of the chamber were found intact. The results showed that the chamber was built later in Bronze Age around 1200 B.C. and was in use until at least 700 B.C. All burials were by cremation and were contained in well-made decorated urns, the earliest of which were Breton in origin and influence. The cremations included pieces of bronze and beads, being possessions of the deceased, one bead of which was made of Egyptian faience which can be dated 1320-1200 B.C. Several urns were intact and examples can be seen in Scilly and Truro Museums.

By the evidence from the above excavations and from other more casual or accidental finds, it is clear that the Bronze Age burials in Scilly took place between the period 2500-700 B.C. Not all the tombs were built at the same time, as shown by the Knackyboy evidence, but the earliest were built around 2500 B.C. when inhumation was the cult. Later in the period, not later than 1200 B.C., cremation became the rule. But whatever the building date of the chambered tombs, it is evident that they were in use for several hundred years.

Concentrations of these tombs can be found on Porthellick Down, St Mary's, North Hill, Samson, and Kittern Hill, Gugh, and were linked in some cases by stone walls. On other exposed moorlands like Shipman Head Down, Bryher, Castle Down, Tresco and Chapel Down, St Martin's, the remains of contemporary field systems can be seen, where small rectilinear fields are defined by boulder walls, stony banks and lynchets. This is presumed to be some form of land division, but the exact nature of the system still remains a mystery.

It is clear that the settlements of the Bronze Age people were situated in the low-lying areas between the islands which are now covered by sea. These would be small groups of round huts, used for living quarters and perhaps shelter for animals. The stone walls still existing on the sea bed, and indeed in some other areas above sea level, are evidence of division of land for the growing of cereals and the grazing of animals. A wealth of evidence from excavations on the islands gives us a fairly clear picture of the Bronze Age way of life.

Perhaps the most complete hut of this period was found on the multi-period site on Nornour, where pottery evidence showed that it was contemporary with the earliest phases of the Knackyboy Tomb, i.e., 1200 B.C. It was oval in shape and measured 22 by 17 ft. The walling existed to a height of 7 ft. and was built of matched granite orthostats 2 ft. by 1 ft. above which were smaller blocks, 8 ins. by 6 ins., set horizontally. The walls were substantial, being 6 ft. in width, and afforded good protection in bad weather. There was a hearth more or less centrally placed, and post holes in the floor at one time probably held roof supports. The construction of the roof is a matter of conjecture, but it was obviously made of perishable material, perhaps wood with interwoven reeds or ferns which were obtainable locally.

Another hut of this period was discovered in 1934 in the bulb garden above Halangy Cliff, St Mary's. This was situated below the better known Bants Carn village site, which was of later date. The foundation of the dwelling revealed a small sub-rectangular hut, which apparently had stone-built drains. This does not comply with the usual type of Bronze Age hut known in the Scillies, but is reputed to be contemporary with the entrance grave complex. Other huts of this period have been found at St Martin's, Bryher and Tean, though less substantial than the Nornour example. At Pernagie Carn, St Martin's, the Rev. H. A. Lewis, a local antiquarian, considered that he had found a potter's workshop, his evidence being based on pottery and

14. Excavations on the site of the Iron Age and Romano-British settlement at Halangy Down, St Mary's.

15. Tooth Rock, Peninnis Head, St Mary's, one of many rocks resembling objects.

16. Pulpit Rock, Old Town Bay,
St Mary's.

17.   The Old Man of Gugh, a single monolith and
      marker stone to a Bronze Age burial.

large quantities of imported clay that were found
on the site.

The economy of these people was based on
mixed farming. Quern stones found in kitchen
middens at Halangy Porth, St Mary's, at Nornour,
at St Martin's and in an entrance grave on Samson,
testify to the growth of cereals. Animal bones found
in the same middens include those of cattle, horse,
sheep and goats, and at English Island Carn, St
Martin's, bones were identified as belonging to a
dwarf species of oxen. This would imply that the
Bronze Age farmers raised a variety of domestic
animals, which formed part of their diet. Bones of
deer and seal were also found at Halangy Porth
amongst the kitchen refuse. Their diet also included
limpets, the shells of which are found in profusion
in all middens, and fish, which although we have
no direct evidence, would obviously have been
freely available from the sea.

The domestic pottery, which was used for both
cooking and storage, was crude and hand-made,
probably made locally. In colour it tends to be
brown or biscuit colour; and granite and mica have
been used in its manufacture. Decoration is simple
and stab marks and cord impression seem to be the
most popular form. Spindle whorls and loom
weights, found at Nornour and St Martin's, indicate

that the weaving of cloth took place in the islands,
probably only for individual requirements.

The discovery of the process for manufacturing
bronze from copper and tin, was the horizon divid-
ing the Bronze Age from the Stone Age. Old stone
artifacts were replaced by metal tools, and these
were produced on a large scale by travelling smiths.
It would appear, however, that the Scilly Isles were
backward in this respect, as the evidence shows
that stone implements were still in use throughout
the later period. All sites have produced a variety
of flint tools, including arrow-heads, hammer stones
and scrapers for use on animal skins. Little bronze
has come to light so far, although fragments have
been found at Knackyboy Cairn and Obadiah's
barrow. These probably represent trade with other
parts of the continent, as do a selection of glass
beads, and the faience also found in the Knackyboy
excavation.

One further group of monuments exists in Scilly
which is attributed to this period. These have a
supposedly religious significance and can be divided
into standing stones, stone rows and henges. The
most well known of the standing stones is the Old
Man of Gugh, featured on the first issue of Gugh
postage stamps, and standing to a height of some
fifteen feet. The purpose of these single stones is
not exactly known, but it has been suggested that
they are either memorials or solitary altars, where
religious ceremonies took place. In 1900 Bonsor
dug to a depth of three feet below the Gugh stone,
in the hope of finding a burial, but his results were
negative. Two other standing stones exist on St
Mary's and a further example was removed at
Longstone after which an area of St Mary's was
named.

Several stone rows have been reported on Scilly,
although many are now incomplete. There is a good
example on the island of Old Man, which is joined
to Tean at low tide. Similar rows exist on Dartmoor. The henge monuments, which are stone
circles, the best known example of which is Stone-
henge in Wiltshire, are similarly depleted in the
Islands. The Rev. Lewis reported two examples on
St Martin's, and Dr Borlase in his survey of the
Islands in 1756 found several on St Mary's, the
largest of which he reports to be 172 feet across.
Today it is difficult to decipher these circles from
random outcrops of granite.

An interesting and unique statue-menhir was
located in recent years on Chapel Down, St Martin's.
The original is now in the Isles of Scilly Museum,
St Mary's, and a replica now stands on the original
site.

18. T.R.H. Prince Charles and Princess Anne at the opening of the Isles of Scilly Museum in 1967.

19. Her Majesty the Queen and Prince Philip in the new Scilly Museum in 1967.

20.

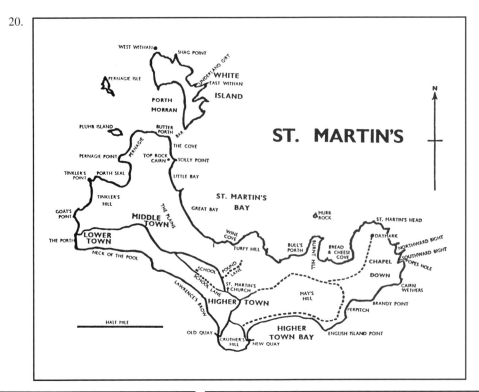

21.   22.

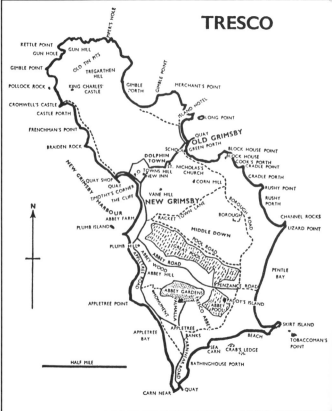

23.

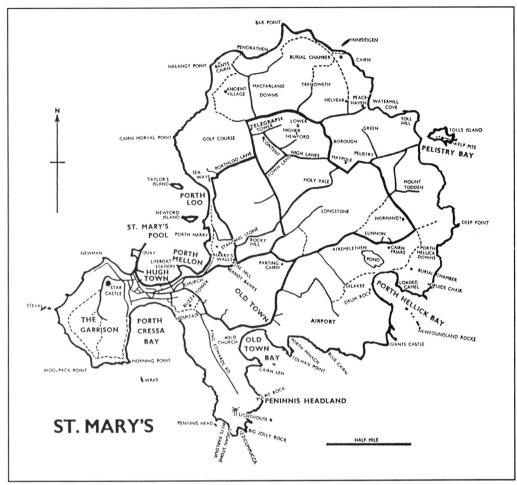

24.

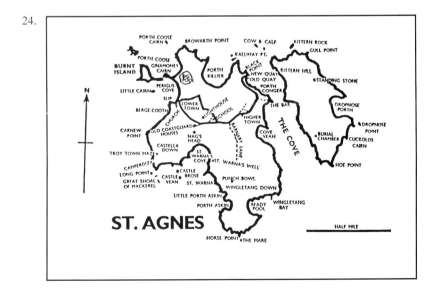

Chapter 2

Natives and Romans

The absence of bronze tools and implements during the Scillonian Bronze Age can be attributed to the lack of skill amongst the inhabitants. Some supplies for the manufacture of bronze were available in Scilly according to Robert Heath, an army officer stationed on the garrison, who stated in 1744 that 'several of the islands afforded tin, and some also lead and copper. The tin is discoverable by the banks next to the sea, where the marks of the ore are in some places visible on the surface'. However, substantial veins of ore are not visible today, although there are signs of early open cast workings on the north downs of Tresco. Certainly tin is plentiful on the Land's End peninsula, which has the same geological structure as Scilly.

There have been several attempts to equate the Scillies with the Cassiterides, a group of islands where it is said that the Phoenicians used to obtain secret supplies of tin before 600 B.C. Strabo, writing in A.D.18, describes these islands as being opposite to the western parts of Britain, and quotes that there are ten in number. He goes on to describe the inhabitants as men in black cloaks who barter tin, lead and skins for earthenware, salt and brazen vessels. If the Scillies are to be identified as the Cassiterides, it is perhaps surprising that no objects associated with the Phoenician culture have been found in the Islands.

Around 700 B.C. a new group of immigrants arrived from Brittany and Western Europe, bringing with them the knowledge of iron working and new types of ceramics which have proved to be the main source of dating for this culture in Scilly. These are known as South West Decorated or Glastonbury wares, and are distinguishable from the earlier pottery, being bowls and jars with burnished exteriors and unusual and stamped decoration. Otherwise the earlier traditions continued in the Islands, with inhabitants still living in circular huts and farming small rectilinear fields. Evidence for this period in Scilly is still very scant, and such excavations that have been carried out have only revealed the use of flint implements. The absence of metal objects once again indicates that Iron Age people of Scilly were backward when compared with their counterparts on mainland Britain.

Evidence for the re-use of Bronze Age dwellings comes from Nornour, where a hut was reconstructed in Early Iron Age style. This took the form of a wheelhouse, similar to those excavated in the Shetland Isles. The main room was divided by stone piers into six peripheral radial compartments, which were entered from the centre of the room. The floor of the room was paved with beach stone and a stone hearth and seat added to the original Bronze Age fittings. A further room, interpreted as a kitchen, was added to the wheelhouse with another hearth and cooking pit and a saddle quern, associated with local farming. A kitchen midden stretching up hill from the seashore contained refuse from several hundred meals. The main constituent was limpet shells, but there were also bones of many animals.

The most impressive monuments to appear in Scilly during this period are the cliff castles; coastal variations of the mainland hill forts. These are the earliest known defences in the Islands and consist of up to three lines of bank and ditch built up from stone and earth across a natural promontory on a cliff top. These small forts, perhaps one acre in size, would have provided adequate defence against would-be raiders. Three castles can be identified in Scilly, the most prominent being Giant's Castle, on the south-east side of St Mary's, which can be clearly seen when landing at St Mary's heliport. Two others at Shipman Head, Bryher and Burnt Hill, St Martin's, make up a trio which are equidistant from one another, on what would have been the outer edge of one large island. These forts may

25.   Giant's Castle, St Mary's, an Iron Age cliff castle. The banks and ditches surrounding the fort are clearly discernible. Dating to about 300 B.C.

26.   Shipman Head Down, Bryher, a prehistoric landscape with Hell Bay on the left. Shipman Head itself is the site of a cliff castle.

27.   Paul Ashbee directs the excavation of a late Iron Age hut at Halangy Down, St Mary's.

28.   A Roundhouse on Nornour, where votive offerings were excavated in large quantities.

reflect tribal divisions in the Islands as they would have been around 300 B.C.

The Roman invasion in A.D.43 brought many changes to Britain, but not to the Isles of Scilly, which remained a cultural backwater. The Romans were mainly interested in what natural resources the new province had to offer, and when building their network of towns came no further west than Exeter, considering Devon and Cornwall of less economic importance apart from supplies of tin or other minerals that were available.

The Roman name for Scilly was Sylina Insula, again inferring that there was only one main island. It was to this place, history records, that two bishops, Instantius and Tiberianus, were exiled in A.D.384. The earliest coin found in Scilly dates to A.D.69, some 26 years after the fall of Britain, and may be an indication that Romanisation reached the Islands quite late. The villages in Scilly, as in Cornwall, show a native existence throughout the Romano-British period, and are a far cry from the villa-farms which sprung up all over the south of England.

Two villages of this period exist in the Islands as well as several odd huts, which have been excavated above and below sea level. Both villages have been laid open for inspection by the visitor, the first being at Halangy Down, St Mary's, better known as Bants Carn ancient village. Some eleven homesteads are positioned on a hillside just above the beach and comprise round, oval and square huts built of well laid granite blocks. Some huts have hearths and a sophisticated system of drainage, and have much in common with the courtyard houses found on the Land's End peninsula at Chysauster and Porthmeor.

During site excavations fragments of high quality Roman pottery such as Samian and Castor wares were located. The diet of the inhabitants included ox, horse, pig, sheep, goat and fish as well as the usual limpets. Spindle whorls found on the site together with slate buttons give some indication of everyday clothing. The houses show several stages of construction from the late Iron Age to the second century A.D.

The other village of this period on the island of Nornour indicates a much earlier settlement. The first group of cairns found on the site date from A.D.69-192 and the second from A.D.262-383. It is known that there was a landfall in the village somewhere around A.D.200, when it is believed that the first phase of occupation ended, and this is borne out by the gap of 70 years in the coin range. Later, in the third century, the site was re-used, perhaps by the inhabitants of the village at Halangy Porth.

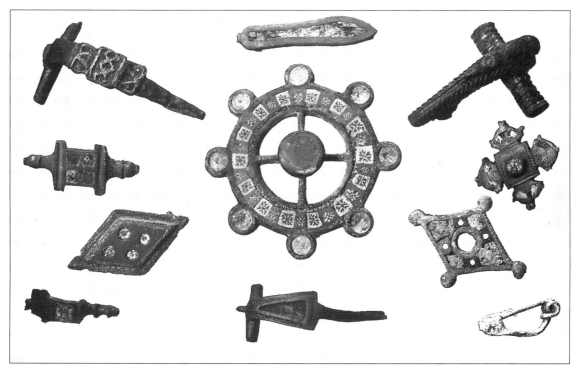

29.   A selection of the brooches from Nornour, now on display in the Isles of Scilly Museum.

During the earliest phase at Nornour, Roman jewellery was manufactured on the site, and the wheelhouse was converted into a finished room and possibly a store, for the import and sale of objects from Western Europe. Some 260 brooches were recovered from the site, together with rings and beads, a large proportion of which can be studied in the Isles of Scilly Museum. Obvious imports to the site include coloured Roman glass and clay figurines from Roman Gaul. The brooches can be divided into 50 types; many are isolated and without parallels. Most of them are hooped and nearly all are decorated with enamel or glass insets. Mr. M. R. Hull suggests that there is a fairly homogenous technique running through the collection and the majority may safely be attributed to one and the same source of manufacture; in other words, they were probably all made at Nornour except perhaps for a few examples used as models.

30.   *(left)* A Roman altar now standing in Tresco Gardens. This was originally found below the Garrison at St Mary's and is believed to be from a Roman temple situated in Hugh Town. The side panels show the raised outlines of a cleaver and a long-shafted axe, both probably sacrificial instruments.

31.   *(below)* A Roman granite column and betrothal stone from Rocky Hill, St Mary's.

The products from Nornour were exported over a wide area; brooches of a similar type have been found on sites all over Britain and distribution probably extends to the Continent also.

Most raw materials for the manufacture of the jewellery were probably imported. Supplies of tin may have been obtained locally, otherwise from Cornwall, whilst copper could have been obtained from Ireland. The glass and beads were probably brought to the site specifically for use as decorative insets. The moulds for the brooches were undoubtedly made from clay and sand, and quantities of these commodities were found in one of the alcoves of the wheelhouse. The activity is believed to have ceased around A.D.200, when the inhabitants may have deserted the site. Seventy years later new settlers moved in and appear to have remained there until very late in the Romano-British period.

Burial of the dead during this period was by crouched inhumation in stone cists, and examples have been found on St Mary's, St Martin's, Samson, Arthur and Old Man. The cist found on Old Man, a small island adjoined to Tean at low tide, contained two brooches of the first century A.D. Similar brooches were found in a cist cemetery excavated in Hugh Town in 1949, a chance discovery made when preparing ground for a council estate. The site revealed 11 oval and rectangular cists built in pits and constructed of granite orthostats, and dry stone walling. Skeletal remains were few, probably due to acid soil, but those found indicate that these were pagan burials. The cemetery appeared to date to the first century A.D.

In sharp contrast with the essentially rural community that we imagine Scilly to have been during the Romano-British period, is the classical altar now standing in Tresco Gardens. This is uninscribed but has side panels bearing reliefs of the long shafted axe and a cleaver. It was originally found at the bottom of Garrison Hill, St Mary's and may have been housed in a Romano-Celtic temple on Mount Holles, below the garrison walls. Many shaped pillars and other stones possibly associated with the temple have been found in Hugh Town and beyond. Some have been built into later walls and buildings, whilst others, like the pillars in the gardens of the *Atlantic Hotel* have been retained for decorative purposes.

Chapter 3

Chapels and Christianity

The period following the withdrawal of the Romans from Britain in the fifth century, has often been referred to as the Dark Ages, mainly because evidence from written sources is scarce, and data from archaeological excavation is equally as elusive. This is the period of the legendary Arthur, when Scilly was reputedly part of the lands of Lyonesse.

Evidence of dwellings in Scilly during the sixth and seventh centuries A.D. is hazy, perhaps because the Islands became a target for Scandinavian raiders who roamed the seas looking for plunder. Such evidence as there is seems to point to the continued use of the Romano-British round houses and not the introduction of rectangular buildings. A continuous occupation of the village at Halangy Down, St Mary's is borne out by the finds of grass-marked pottery. A kitchen midden of the periods built above the cist cemetery in Hugh Town, revealed that limpets were still the main source of food, together with fish, ox, horse, sheep, pig, rabbit and common frog.

Most evidence from the period before the Norman Conquest in 1066 comes from graveyards

32.   The remaining arches of St Nicholas' Priory, located within the Tresco sub-tropical gardens.

and religious sites in Scilly. Christianity arrived in Britain in A.D.597 when St Augustine and other missionaries arrived on the scene, but when it reached Scilly is still a matter of conjecture. The earliest evidence is from a sixth-century tombstone built into the later priory church on Tresco, inscribed '... THI FILI ... COGVI'. This Latin inscription incorporates Celtic personal names and may be associated with a nearby cist cemetery. Close by in a part of Tresco Abbey Gardens are three early graves perhaps dating to the eighth century, measuring between four and six feet in length with a covering stone slab. The orientation to the east suggests that they contained Christian burials, and this is substantiated by the fact that a stone with a simple cross was located nearby. The finds on Tresco may indicate that a monastic settlement of an early date preceded St Nicholas' Priory, founded in the 11th century.

Elsewhere in Scilly five other christian cist cemeteries have been identified, each associated with rectangular stone chapels aligned east-west with a doorway on the south side. Three of these on St Helen's, Tean and St Martin's have survived in a state of ruin, whilst others may have stood on St Mary's, St Agnes and Samson where cemeteries have been recorded. Prior to knowledge of the submergence these religious foundations were

33. The monk's cell in the St Helen's hermitage complex.

interpreted as hermitages, located on separate islands, but now that it appears that there was one large land mass at the time, they may well have served as early parish churches.

One of them, which may still qualify as a hermitage is on the island of St Helen's, which, despite its name, is dedicated to St Elidius. Here amongst the bracken can be seen the remains of a religious complex which comprises a church, an

34. An imaginative reconstruction of Norsemen visiting St Elid on the island at St Helen's, as recorded in *Heimskringla.*

35.   All Saints', Bryher, built in 1742 in a cruciform pattern.

36.   St Agnes' church, erected in 1821.

oratory, three rectangular huts, a round cell and a well, all enclosed within a stone compound. All these features with the exception of the church, were built before the Norman Conquest. The oratory is a single-chambered rectangular building with a doorway in the south wall. A stone altar and relic holder are situated against the east wall. The church, which lies just below the oratory, shows three phases of building. The final phase which occurred in the 12th century, enclosed a significant grave, perhaps that of the founder of the settlement. Two other graves contained the remains of four other people.

An event which may be connected with the settlement on St Helen's and indeed Saint Elidius is recorded in the *Orkneyinga Saga* for the years A.D.991-94, and written of by the 13th-century writer, Snorri Sturluson. It tells of the Norse King Olaf Trygvesson, and his journey to England. He first sailed to Northumberland where he plundered, and then to the Hebrides where he fought some battles. He continued to the Isle of Man, Ireland, Wales and Cumberland and finally to Northern France, leaving a trail of destruction. When he left France, intending to sail for England, he came across the Scilly Isles, lying westward from England in the ocean. While Olaf was in Scilly, he heard of a fortune teller in the Islands who could foresee the future, and in whom many believed. Being a curious man, he decided to try this man's gift of prophecy.

He sent for one of the most handsome and strongest of his followers, clothed him magnificently, and bade him visit the fortune teller and declare that he was the king. When the messenger reached the fortune teller and presented himself as the king he received the answer, 'Thou art not the king, but I advise thee to be faithful to thy king'.

When the man returned and told Olaf, he was even more curious and visited the fortune teller himself. He asked him if he could foresee his future and was told:

> Thou wilt become a renowned king, and do celebrated deeds. Many men will thou bring to faith and baptism, and both to they own and others good; and that thou mayst have no doubt of the truth of this answer, listen to these tokens: When thou comest to thy ships, many of thy people will conspire against thee, and then a battle will follow in which many of thy men will fall, and thou will be wounded almost to death, and carried upon a shield to thy ship; yet after seven days thou shalt be well of they wounds, and immediately thou shall let thyself be baptised.

In the events that followed the meeting, the fortune teller's prophecy came true and Olaf was wounded and recovered seven days later. Olaf returned to him and asked him how he came to have such wisdom in foretelling the future. The hermit replied that the Christian God let him know all that he desired, and brought before Olaf many other proofs of the power of the Almighty. In consequence Olaf allowed himself to be baptised, and ordered that his followers be baptised also. When he returned to his native country he spread the word of Christianity throughout the land.

Whether the hermit referred to in the story is Saint Elidius, or a resident at the settlement on St Helen's, is a matter of conjecture, but the fact remains that Scilly played its part in spreading Christianity at an early date.

On the adjacent island of Tean a rectangular oratory, in association with five early Christian graves was excavated in 1956. Grass-marked pottery

37. A statue menhir or celtic idol on Chapel Down, St Martin's. It is believed to be the head and shoulders of a human and may date to any time between the Bronze Age and the Romano-Celtic period. It was first located in the 1940s and then lost until found again 50 years later.

38. Young children at the holy well dedicated to St Warna on the island of St Agnes. The saint was thought to have the power of attracting shipwrecks. Three steps lead down to an underground chamber.

found on the site dated the building to around A.D.700. This was believed to be a sanctuary dedicated to Sancta Theona. In 1971, excavations on the island of Samson just above the beach level, revealed another series of early Christian graves dating from the early sixth century, and continuing into the medieval period. The earlier graves had an edging of small granite slabs, and the latter an additional kerb and a marker stone. Two buildings of the earlier phases were also found on the site. The earliest building had walls made of wattle which were supported by wooden posts at the corners and at the entrance, where a threshold stone was found in position. It was rectangular in shape and measured eleven feet by eight feet and contained two hearths edged in beach pebbles, which had a diameter of two feet six inches. At a slightly later date a stone building was erected seven feet to the north, which may have been part of a complex dedicated to St Samson.

Medieval documents refer to a chapel of St Maudut, identified as standing below the garrison in Hugh Town, St Mary's, remains of which no longer survive. Similarly on the island of St Agnes we must rely on documentation for a possible chapel dedicated to Sancta Warna above the old harbour of Periglis. John Leland reports that there was a chapel here by 1540, which was destroyed by Parliamentary forces in the Civil War. The 1652 Parliamentary Survey confirms this as the site of both a chapel and a burial ground. Reports of human bones and skulls being found in a low cliff south west of the lifeboat slip have also been recorded. St Warna's holy well on St Agnes is probably a medieval structure, but the tradition of attributing supernatural powers to water originated in the pre-Christian era.

The layout of the chapel on Chapel Down, St Martin's can be made out in times of drought. It lies adjacent to the Daymark, and as it has no associated burials may well be a lighthouse chapel where a fire beacon was maintained.

Chapter 4

The First Communities

Some sort of social organisation came to the Islands shortly after the Norman Conquest in 1066, when Scilly became the property of the Crown. From 1141 it was part of the Earldom, and then after 1337 was vested in the Duchy of Cornwall. Administration of Tresco and Bryher, one land mass under the name of Renteman and later St Nicholas, was under the control of Tavistock Abbey, which by a charter of 1120 established St Nicholas' Priory, the ruins of which can still be seen in Tresco Gardens. Meanwhile the islands now represented by St Mary's and St Agnes were in lay hands, notably the de Wika family, who formed the first major settlement at Old Town, St Mary's.

The settlement and harbour of Old Town can probably be said to be at least one thousand years old. The name itself indicates an ancient origin even though it did not come into use until the 17th century. At that time a new settlement was forming below Star Castle on the Hugh, first to be called New Towne and later Hugh Town. As the original settlement began to lose its importance, it took on the title of 'Old Town' to differentiate it from its new neighbour that had sprung up on the sand bar at the other side of Penninis Head.

To appreciate fully the origins of the Old Town settlement it is necessary to examine its geographical position relative to the land mass of Scilly. Before

39.   A fleet of boats in St Mary's Roads at the turn of the century.

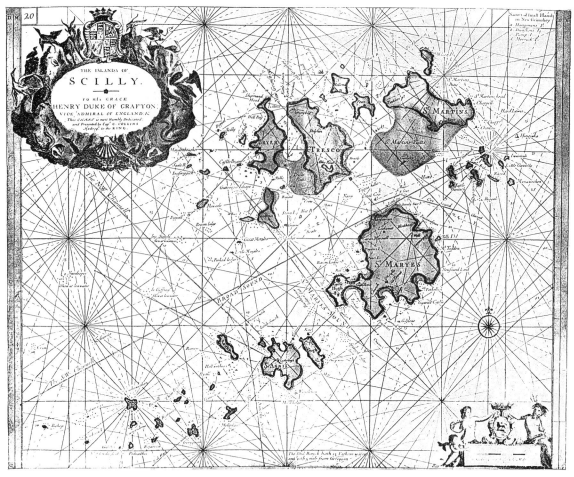

40. A map produced for Henry Duke of Grafton, c.1750.

the seventh century A.D., Scilly, with the exception of the St Agnes Group, was one large island existing under the name of En-Noer (or Ennor). Between the 7th and the 13th centuries the rising sea level gradually submerged the low-lying areas and formed the island archipelago as we see it today. Throughout this whole sequence of submergence, Old Town Bay, situated as it was on the outside of the main island, was unaffected by the change and remained a natural harbour with deep water access.

Documentary evidence dated around 1150 of a grant to Tavistock Abbey by Reginald, Earl of Cornwall, shows that even by this late period the islands had not taken their present shape. Islands specified in the document were Rentemen (Tresco and Bryher), Nurcho (St Martin's and the Eastern Isles), St Helen's, Samson and Tean. Only those islands that were in monastic hands and administered by the Prior of Scilly were listed. The remaining islands were described as Ennor (St Mary's) and Aganas (St Agnes) in another document dated 1199, when the secular owner and proprietor was Richard de Wika, whose family were from north Cornwall. The name Ennor, then, which had originally been used to encompass all the main islands when they were one land mass, was now being used to describe the island of St Mary's only, presumably because the majority of the population lived there. The name St Mary's, in the form of Insula Sancte Marie, first occurs in 1375, undoubtedly from the dedication of the church in Old Town.

Certainly by the 12th century Old Town was the main settlement and harbour on Ennor (St Mary's) and probably the whole island group. The village itself was not easily detectable from the open sea or, indeed, approachable by large ships as the water in the harbour would have been too shallow. The first mention of the settlement seems to have been in 1151 when the *Orkneyinga Saga* records that three notable Vikings sailed from Orkney to Syllingar (Scilly), won a fight, and took much plunder at Mariuhofn. This name is in Old Norse and translates as Mary's Haven, and as the raiders were looking for church fittings the Saga is obviously describing a raid on the church at Old Town. In the 13th century Tavistock Abbey refers to the settlement as La Val (Norman French for 'At the bottom'), a name which is often wrongly linked with Holy Vale, which lies one mile from the village. Later came the title Porthenor, translating as the porth or landing place for Ennor, which may have coincided with the building of a quay. Before 1700 the name Porth-Eglos (Church Bay) was being used and by 1708 when Gosselo made his map of Scilly this had been corrupted to Pereglis, a name still in use on St Agnes to describe a harbour with a church. Soon after, Hugh Town became firmly established and the present title of Old Town (Bay) came into use.

The attractive little church in Old Town, now only used occasionally for services, is the oldest of the Island churches still standing. From the earliest days all the churches were under the control of Tavistock Abbey which received its charter in A.D.891. In about the year 1120, Henry I granted to Abbot Osbert 'all the churches of Scilly with the appurtenances' and this was to be administered by Turold, then Prior of Scilly. St Nicholas' Priory was the home of the Prior and his monks. The Prior also held most of the land in Scilly with the exception of Ennor and Aganas which were in lay hands. Despite this, the Abbey had control of the churches on these two islands which included that of St Mary in Old Town.

The aforementioned sortee by the Vikings in the year 1151 to 'Mary's Haven' to collect church plate indicates that the building was in existence at that time. Experts suggest a building date somewhere between 1130 and 1140. Little of this original church now survives except perhaps for a reshaped Norman arch as one enters the nave from the porch. The cross that was erected on the east gable summit in 1887, however, is believed to date back to the 13th century. In the 19th century it was one of two that still marked the extent of the glebe

41.   St Mary's church, Old Town, St Mary's, the earliest surviving church in the Islands. Erected between 1130 and 1140, the north and south aisles were added in the 17th century. It was rebuilt in the 1830s and restored in 1890.

42. Old Town churchyard, St Mary's, which contains the graves of many old Scillonians and shipwreck victims, including the many dead from the SS *Schiller* disaster. Two prominent obelisks are memorials to Augustus Smith and Louise Holzmaister, a passenger lost from the SS *Schiller.*

lands which brought in income to support the church and chaplain. The one on the church was removed from a hedge in a lane called High Cross, and the other was identified later in the garden of Rocky Hill.

The church as it appears today consists mainly of 17th-century architecture, with five rectangular windows of the period. This work began in 1660 when it was almost completely rebuilt for the use of the soldiers on the Garrison. The porch displays a date of 1662 and the north aisle is recorded as being built in the same year. The south aisle was added in 1677. Use of the church by the army is confirmed by Borlase in 1752 when he wrote that 'the soldiers of the Garrison have a gallery allocated to them in this church facing the Commanding Officer, who has a handsome seat below in the chancel'. The gallery no longer exists but its supports can be detected on the south wall.

The situation had completely changed when Spry visited in 1800 and reported that 'the old church hath been suffered to go out of repair and part is fallen down, and no divine service hath been

performed there for the last two years'. After this it would seem that for some long period the building stayed in a state of disrepair, during which time it was used as a mortuary chapel. Restoration took place again in 1890 leaving the church much as we see it today.

One hundred yards north of the village is a rocky crag on which Ennor Castle once stood. By the nature and shape of the rock the structure was irregular in plan, 13 by 18 metres in area, with a defensive stone wall running around the summit of the crag. The castle was built to accommodate the Constable and Keeper of the Isles of Scilly who looked after the general secular administration of the Islands and acted as tenant-in-chief for the King.

The actual building date of the structure is not known, but the first mention was in a deed of 1244 when it was termed 'Castrum de Enoer'. Secular authority in the Islands, however, was vested in the Earls of Cornwall by the time of Henry I (1100-35), and by 1176 Richard de Wika of Week St Mary, in north Cornwall, owned Ennor (St Mary's) and Aganas (St Agnes). His son, Richard, took over

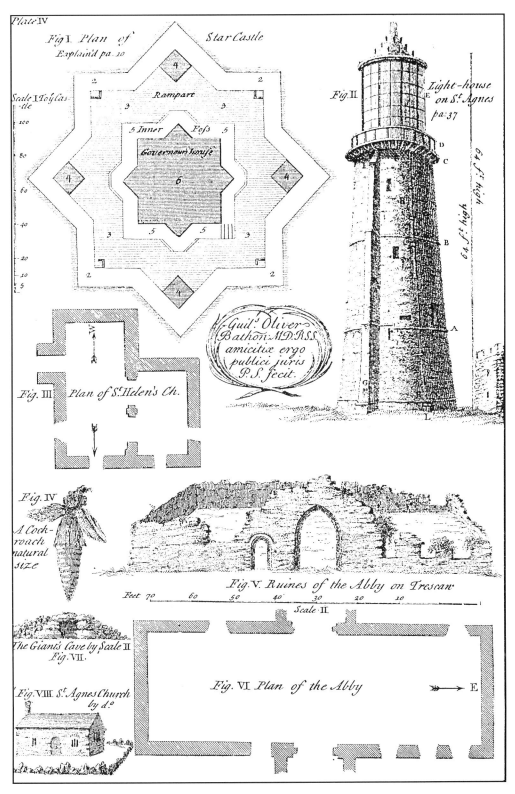

43.   A selection of Scilly buildings as seen by William Borlase in 1756.

in 1199 as proprietor of the same area. These early appointments of governorship, if the tenants were resident in the Islands, suggest that the Castle may have been in existence in the mid-12th century.

From 1248 to 1251 Dreux de Barrentine, a Norman knight, was appointed Governor of Scilly, and supplied an armed garrison of men at Ennor Castle in exchange for his landholding. Before 1300 Edward I had appointed Ranulph de Blanchminster of Benamy in north Cornwall as tenant. His duties were to supply 12 armed men, keep the peace and pay a rent of 300 puffins or six shillings and eightpence each year at Michaelmas. At this time puffins were greatly valued as food and for their feathers. However, this rent was always paid in money form until 1547. Ranulph was licensed to crenellate the Castle in 1315 and died in 1348.

Walter Hull was Constable of the Castle in 1353, after which the Black Prince appointed William de Morier. The tenancy then went to the Tresillions, the Coleshills and the Arundells until finally, in 1505, John Crocker, the husband of Anne Arundell, became 'tenant-in-chief of the castle and manor of Scilly'. The Castle by this time was on

the decline and by 1540 when Leland visited the Islands it was starting to deteriorate, although he described it as a 'meately [moderately] strong pile'. With the rise of Star Castle on the Hugh and to some extent the placing of the unfinished Harry's Walls, Ennor Castle became a ruin.

The building was dismantled and the stone used to reinforce cottages in Old Town. The re-use of stone in Scilly is a common occurrence, and it has been suggested that, when Ennor Castle was originally constructed, stone was brought down from Giant's Castle, an Iron Age promontory fort situated on the cliff near the airport.

Some fragments of the castle still survive today, well hidden in the undergrowth on the rocky crag, but there is no public access to this ancient monument which was once the most important residence in Scilly.

Within the harbour can be seen the remains of the medieval quay which was used regularly when Old Town was the principal settlement on St Mary's. There is no specific dating for the structure which over the years has been repaired and rebuilt after storm damage and natural erosion from the sea. It

44.   The remaining ramparts of Ennor Castle, Old Town, as they were at the turn of the century.

45.   Star Castle, Hugh Town and the harbour in 1756.

46.   St Mary's Quay, *c.*1926, with a group of geology students about to go for a sail.

47. *(left)* Buzza Tower, St Mary's, *c.*1880. As a windmill the tower replaced Penninis mill in 1834. In 1912 it was called King Edward's Tower and was maintained as a memorial to his visit.

48. *(above)* The remains of a granite mill on the Middle Down, St Mary's, believed by the author to have been used for cider manufacture, but its function is unproven.

49.   The base of a ruined windmill on Penninis Head, St Mary's. This was built in 1726 for civilian use, and was reported by Troutbeck to be the only grist mill in 1796. By 1798 the Scillonian poet Robert Maybee was the miller, and it continued in use until 1834.

50. Building the original quay on St Martin's.

51. The quay, St Martin's after excessive storm damage.

52.   An old thatched cottage on Bryher.

53.   Old Town, St Mary's in 1884 showing typical Scillonian thatched granite cottages.

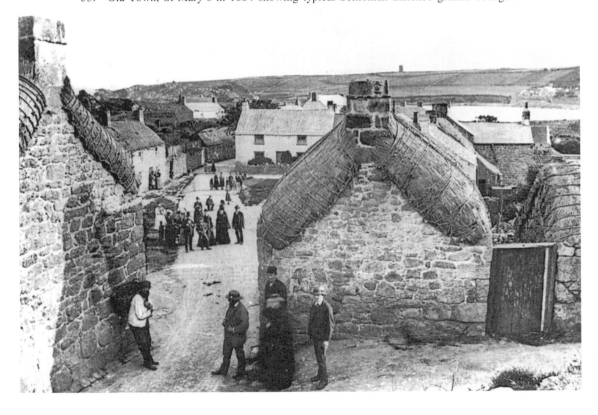

54. Houses at Old Grimsby, Tresco, in the 1880s.

can be assumed that some sort of quay was in existence in the 13th century to receive goods and supplies destined for the castle, and its usage would have declined in the 17th century when the new quay was built in Hugh Town.

The entrance to the harbour is shallow and could not have accommodated large ships, although there are reports of medium-sized vessels docking alongside the quay to load kelp for Bristol. In 1752 Borlase described it as a 'poor little pier', which is an indication that it was going out of use at that time. The small jetty placed at right angles to the main quay was added to give additional shelter to small boats and make running lines unnecessary. In 1856 there were the remains of a further jetty known as 'John Smith's Quay' after a farmer who had land to the west of Old Town.

By the mid-19th century there was a shed to house the pilot gig within the harbour, and part of

its foundations can still be detected. A wooden slipway supported by oak posts carried the boat down to the water. This was probably not there in 1820 when Robert Maybee, the Scillonian poet, remembered seeing 'a large pilot boat, two six-oared gigs and eight smaller boats moored in the bay'. Maybee lived on Peninnis Head where his father worked on the windmill, of which only the base now remains. When the windmill was dismantled it is believed that the stones were used to repair Old Town Quay.

Although Old Town was the main settlement in the Islands, documentary evidence and medieval finds indicate that there were other smaller villages, at Churchtown and Lower Town, St Martin's, Old Grimsby and Borough Farm on Tresco, Norrard and Southard on Bryher, and Middle Town on St Agnes. Others might still lie undetected under modern housing.

Chapter 5

The Island Fortress

Ecclesiastical control in the Islands had dwindled by the 16th century and ceased after 1539 when the Tavistock lands were surrendered to Henry VIII. The disappearance of the monks affected the lives of the inhabitants by depriving them of employment and an outlet for their produce. By all accounts the Islands had degenerated by the time of the dissolution, and this is confirmed by John Leland, the antiquarian who visited the Scillies in 1548. His visit appears hurried and his notes scant, but he gives a rough description of the 'defaced and worn'

Ennor Castle, and the 'poor cell of the monks of Tavistock' on Tresco. Of the population he recorded that 'few men be glad to inhabit these islets, for all the plenty, for robbers by sea that take their catail by force. The robbers be Frenchmen and Spaniards'.

Leland also records that Davers and Whitington, two gentlemen from Wiltshire and Gloucestershire were the owners of Scilly at the time of his visit. However, war with France had led to the construction of many new defences around the southern coast of England, and the strategic importance of

55.   Harry's Walls, St Mary's, an unfinished fort begun in 1551 to protect St Mary's harbour. Only the south west side was completed due to bad siting.

56. The Blockhouse, Old Grimsby, Tresco, constructed in 1554 to protect St Helen's Pool. In 1652 it was listed as Dover Fort.

Scilly at the entrance of the Western Approaches was realised. A government agreement was made with the town of Plymouth to fortify St Nicholas' Island (Tresco) and the Lord Admiral Seymour took over on behalf of the Crown. In 1549 he was accused of using the Islands as a base for piracy and plotting against the king. He was beheaded by order of Edward VI. In the same year a Mr. Godolphin was appointed Captain of the Islands, and their family connection continued with scarcely an interruption for 282 years.

Fortification of the Islands began during the reign of Edward VI, and provided work for the Scillonians. One of the first forts was Harry's Walls, wrongly attributed to Henry VIII, as the name infers. In 1551, the Privy Council sent a letter to one John Killigrew ordering him to 'make a fort in our Ladies Isle (St Mary's) at Scilly upon the little hill betwixt the fresh water and St Mary's Road'. There was also to be a brewhouse and a horsemill. The siting of the fort on Mount Flagon was to ensure the safety of the harbour from would be invaders, but the erection of the fortification was never completed. At Hatfield House there is a plan of the building as it was meant to be which bears the legend:

This fortress begonne in oure ladies ilande for the defence of the whole Isles, and not finished, the timberwork for the same already framed for the setting up, with a brewhouse and milne lying in South Wales, redy to be conveyed to the said Iles when order may be given as touching the same.

The plan shows a square fort with an acutely pointed bastion at each corner, with an overall measurement of the square of 130 feet.

Other buildings erected between 1548 and 1554 included King Charles' Castle and two blockhouses on Tresco, with a third on the north east coast of St Mary's. King Charles Castle is another misnomer, created to guard New Grimsby Harbour and the Tresco Channel. Its siting on the North Downs of Tresco was probably a mistake as the fort never proved to be efficient, even though it covered a wide field of fire. Legend has it that the guns had to be tilted to such a degree that cannon balls would not stay in the barrels and rolled down into the sea! The surviving ruins show a large area of living quarters as well as the gun platform. During the later Civil War a large earthwork defence was added to the castle which can be detected to the north and east of the ruins.

57.   The entrance to Star Castle, built for Elizabeth I by Francis Godolphin in 1593. The building takes the shape of an eight-pointed star.

58.   Lower Benham Battery, the Garrison, St Mary's, with the Trinity House buildings used to accommodate lighthouse keepers in Scilly.

59.   One of two water tanks standing outside the parish church on St Mary's. These bear the arms of George II and the date 1727, and are believed to have originally stood outside Star Castle.

On the opposite side of Tresco the Old Block-house was built at the same time to guard the approaches to Old Grimsby harbour and St Helen's Pool. It comprised a rectangular stone platform which was reached by stone steps on the western side. In 1652 it was known as Dover Fort and was fairly modest, with meagre living quarters for its garrison. Other banks and ditches in the vicinity may indicate that it was extended during the Civil War.

Cromwell's Castle, which is sited on the water's edge below King Charles' Castle, was built at the end of the Civil War in 1651 as a defence against an attack from the Dutch. It was named in honour of Oliver Cromwell, although the title came at a later date. It comprised a tower and a platform, the latter being an addition made by Master Gunner Abraham Tovey in the mid-18th century. The plat-form had six gun ports, which were splayed to allow movement of the guns. Stone for its building came from the ruins of King Charles'Castle on the promontory above.

Henry VIII maintained a garrison at Ennor Castle from 1544-7, and during Edward VI's reign it continued to defend Old Town harbour, being used as an armoury for the 150 men posted in Scilly. During the early part of Elizabeth I's reign the defences ran down as, surprisingly enough, the Queen made no special provision against the Spanish Armada of 1588. However, in 1570 she leased the Islands to Francis Godolphin for a term of 38 years at an annual rent of £20. The continued war with Spain eventually resulted in the fortification of the Hugh, an island joined to St Mary's by a sand bar, which overlooked the main harbour. It was on this sand bar that the present settlement of Hugh Town began to develop soon after 1600, replacing the original capital at Old Town.

The principal new fortification was Star Castle built in 1593. Godolphin himself appointed Robert Adams, an engineer, to supervise the works and to help with its design and siting. From the air, the castle takes on the shape of an eight-pointed star and was built inside a moat over which was a stone bridge and portcullis. The building had a basement for storage, two floors of accommodation for the garrison and a curtain with guardhouses. Around 1600 a stretch of curtain wall was built across the neck of the Hugh from Jeffersons to Lower Benham Battery with three sally ports. At a similar time Godolphin began the construction of a quay for the new harbour at St Mary's Pool.

60.   Cromwell's Castle from King Charles' Castle, looking towards Bryher. This fortified tower was built in 1651 in honour of Oliver Cromwell at a time when the Islands were threatened by the Dutch fleet.

NEW GRYNSEY. *1 Shipman Head. 2 Part of Brehar. 3 Hangman Island. 4 Town of Brehar. 5 Part of Oliver's Camp. 6 Oliver's Castle. 7 Old Castle. 8 The Battery.*

Car: Lyttelton L.L.D. R.S.S. Dec.r Exon: pro amore quo hæccine semper fovebat Studia Portulum hunc nec inamœnum insculpi P.S. voluit

61.   New Grimsby harbour in 1756.

62.   King Charles' Castle, Castle Down, Tresco. Erected between 1550 and 1554 to cover the entrance to New
      Grimsby harbour, it eventually went out of use when replaced by Cromwell's Castle.

63.   A stretch of curtain wall erected around the Garrison between 1715 and 1742.

During the Civil War, the Isles of Scilly were in Royalist hands, and were used for raids on Parliamentary shipping. Parliament tended to ignore the Islands until 1651, when the presence of the Dutch fleet spurred them into action. Admiral Blake was sent to capture the Islands and, instead of attacking St Mary's, he tactically anchored in St Helen's Pool and fought his way on to Tresco. At Oliver's Battery, Crow Point he placed guns with which he could bombard St Mary's Pool at long range. Eventually the Royalists were defeated and Scilly fell into Parliamentary hands. Cromwell's Castle was built at this time in honour of the General.

During the Civil War, the Royalists had erected many new earthworks and fortifications to protect the Islands. These mainly consisted of earthern ditches and banks with little stone work in existence. St Mary's was protected by batteries on Toll's Island, Bar Point, Carn Morval and Penninis Head. Meanwhile on the Hugh there is evidence of continuous breastwork on the line of the present stone wall, and of a similar earthwork running between Toll's Island and Bar Point.

After the restoration of the monarchy in 1660, the Godolphin family once more became the proprietors of Scilly and remained so until 1831, when the Duke of Leeds refused to renew the lease to the Crown. The Scillonians, who had first profited from the monks and then from the soldiers, were now beginning to know poverty. The fortifications themselves had become run-down and this was confirmed in a report issued by Colonel Christian Lily in 1715 about the state of the defences on the Hugh. As a result of the report a period of building commenced which continued until 1746.

For the next 31 years work was carried out which resulted in the Hugh being turned into a formidable bastion and the whole island being known as the Garrison, a name that it carries today. The main curtain wall was rebuilt and extended around most of the headland, and was capable of mounting 120 guns. The sea approaches were covered by batteries in large bastions mainly at Morning Point, Woolpack Point and south of Steval Point; Charles' Battery and Newman's Platform covered the north side.

Newman House, which is adjacent to the platform, was the Garrison stores and dates to c.1716-18. The magazine, just inside the main gate, also dates from this time. The main Garrison Gate

64. Garrison Gate, St Mary's showing the initials A.T. after Abraham Tovey, the master gunner on the fortification. It was erected in 1742.

is originally an Elizabethan structure, despite the 1742 date shown below the bell parapet with inscribed stones showing the initials of King George, Francis Godolphin and Abraham Tovey, the master gunner. It was the latter who was mainly responsible for all these works.

In the 1890s Scilly was classed as a defended port, and four batteries were built to withstand attack from enemy cruisers and U-boats. Various additions were made during both World Wars when the garrison accommodated hundreds of servicemen.

Chapter 6

A Living from the Sea

As one might expect with a group of islands surrounded by the Atlantic Ocean, the lives of the inhabitants have always been ruled by the sea, and a large number of stone relics still in existence bear witness to the fact that the Scillonians turned to the sea for survival in times of hardship and famine. Many such periods occurred during the Islands' history, the only major source of employment being the erection of fortifications.

Fish was naturally an important source of food in Scilly, but fishing was never at any time a major industry in the Islands. During the periods of economic depression the islanders disregarded the commercial possibilities, their main concern being to feed themselves. Anyway, the fish markets on the mainland were inaccessible to the people of Scilly, who were not in a position to own boats of the required size. Any man who owned a dinghy

65.   The Old Quay at Old Town first mentioned in 1554 in connection with Ennor Castle, but possibly much older. In the foreground is the fish salting trough used to cure pilchards, which may have originally been a coffin.

66.   Jacob Deason, and his wife, of St Agnes in 1895. He was referred to as 'an old smuggler'.

67.   The Old Customs House in 1880. This building is now the *Atlantic Hotel*.

in Scilly would have been considered well off.

However, ling caught on long lines and dried and salted was apparently exported in a small way and well thought of, as is testified by a letter from Lord Nelson to a friend in Plymouth in 1803 thanking him for the Scilly ling. Two attempts to established fisheries both ended in failure. In 1819 attempts were made to start a mackerel and pilchard fishery, and to this end cellars were set up on Tresco for storing and curing the fish. A later attempt by the Lord Proprietor, T. A. Dorrien-Smith to catch pilchards on a commercial scale ended in disaster because of misunderstandings between the fishermen and merchants.

During the 19th century, limited attempts were made to export shellfish which included crayfish, lobsters, limpets and shrimps, which were collected by a Southampton merchant. A more lucrative time occurred when Scilly was made a rendezvous for a mackerel fishery and St Mary's Quay was the scene of regular fish auctions with numerous Newlyn boats standing by to transport the mackerel to market. One relic of the old fishery days is to be found on the east side of Old Town Bay, where a large stone trough, perhaps originally an ancient coffin, was once used for the communal salting of fish, mainly pilchards. This was certainly in use in 1796 when the Rev. Troutbeck wrote about it and commented that 'stages were erected in a field adjoining for drying the fish in the sun'.

The period of near famine in Scilly was mainly between the years 1742 and 1834 and, besides fishing, the other main activities to which the Scillonians resorted were smuggling and kelp-making. The Islands were well situated for the former activity and many large vessels passed close by. It was not unusual for islanders to row out in their fast gigs under cover of darkness to barter with an East Indiaman or the like. On these expeditions, which they regarded as fair trade, they could obtain tea, sugar, tobacco and cognac in exchange for mundane items like potatoes. Their sole enemy was the resident exciseman who had the near impossible task of having to cover all the islands. Robbing the exchequer was not considered to be a crime and even the Rev. Troutbeck, Chaplain of the Isles, was

68.   Jim Nance, his wife and seven daughters at their home at Bleak House, St Martin's. His ancestors started the kelp industry in Scilly.

69. Two Scillonian women burning seaweed during a kelp-making ceremony.

70. A kelp pit on White Island, off St Martin's, used to make soda-ash from seaweed.

71.   A Scillonian lady spinning wool.

found to be involved in a smuggling ring after he had earlier written 'of late years spiritous liquors are so cheap that the poorest persons can purchase them to the injury of their health, the promotion of idleness and the loss of the public revenue'.

Today there is still much evidence of this activity which had its heyday in the late 18th century. There are rusty bolts embedded in the granite at high water where the smugglers moored, and cellars and caches in many of the cottages around Old Grimsby at Tresco where the contraband was stored. Eventually, the loss of revenue caused the Government to provide Revenue boats to patrol the island waters, and the Customs men introduced a rule that only four men at a time could be present in a rowing boat, which prevented gigs and other vessels from travelling long distances. The Golden Age of smuggling was over, but the activity continued on a smaller scale and probably still does.

After the exodus of the military forces in 1667, the islanders were at their lowest ebb and became a classless community, living a subsistence economy with little leadership and guidance. It was in 1684 that James Nance came to the islands and introduced the manufacture of soda-ash from seaweed on the island of Tean. Kelp-making as an industry was totally labour intensive with no overheads, a situation which appealed to those islanders with little or no resources. All they needed was a kelp pit—a depression in the ground surrounded with stones—in which they could burn seaweed to produce an ash extensively used in the manufacture of glass, soap and alum.

Seaweed was freely available around the islands and was gathered daily by the whole family. When the weed was dry it was burnt in kelp pits to obtain ash, and at the same time gave off an obnoxious smell, which often spread right across the Islands. Most of the time the Scillonians laboured hard for almost negligible returns, and suffered from lung infections and pneumonia from the continual wearing of wet clothing. It took a man, his wife and four children two weeks to make one ton of ash, and the average quantity produced annually by one family was around 10 tons, which brought in £10 per annum. To make this amount it was necessary for the family to collect and carry 264 tons of wet seaweed, mostly on their backs. It was no wonder that the mortality rate was high.

Marketing of the product was handled by the middlemen and merchants who shipped the soda-ash to Bristol and Gloucester for use in manufacture. The existence of middlemen often resulted in

72.   Augustus Smith with the St Agnes pilots, c.1871.

the exploitation of the islanders, as in the case of the Steward of the Islands who gave the kelpers 20 shillings a ton when the merchants were paying 44 shillings. As the people were all tenants they ran the risk of being turned out of their holding if they attempted to sell their kelp elsewhere. During the Napoleonic Wars of 1799-1815 kelp sold well but new chemical processes and improvements in communications gradually led to the downfall of the industry which ceased in Scilly by 1835.

Another activity which helped the economy of the islanders was piloting. The position of Scilly at the apex of the Bristol and English Channels meant that large transatlantic vessels had to pass close to the treacherous rocks of the archipelago. If a big sea was running or the area was blanketed with fog, the captain would require the services of a pilot who would either guide the ship through the maze of rocks or into the shelter of the islands. The Scillonians were happy to provide this service at a price, and were even happier if the vessel anchored off St Mary's, as there was always a chance of bartering goods with them.

The larger boats used to land pilots on a vessel were 30 ft. pilot cutters, decked with tall masts. These were usually accompanied by the smaller pilot gigs, all purpose vessels, rowed by a crew of six with a small sail. These versatile slim boats could cut through the waves at speed and were often rowed over long distances. Most of the off-islanders had their own gigs and crews comprising farmers, labourers and fishermen who, like a lifeboat crew, had to be available at a moment's notice. When a 'jack' was spotted, which was a flag indicating that a pilot's services were needed, the race was on to see which gig could reach the vessel first to acquire the job and the financial reward which followed.

This rivalry between gig crews is still reflected in the Friday night gig races which are held on St Mary's during the summer between the vessels belonging to the different islands. Whilst gigs are still built in the islands, many of those currently in use are of an ancient nature, like the *Bonnet* (1830) and the *Golden Eagle* (1870) which carry crews from St Mary's, the *Shah* (1873), the St Agnes gig, whilst the *Czar* (1879), which takes a crew of eight, represents Tresco and Bryher.

Scilly pilots were always equal to their task, and had the knowledge of the local waters which had been handed down from father to son. However, the gigs were most needed when the weather was bad and the seas mountainous. Many craft were turned over and the crews dashed against the rocks

73.   The weekly gig race on Scilly, in vessels once used for piloting.

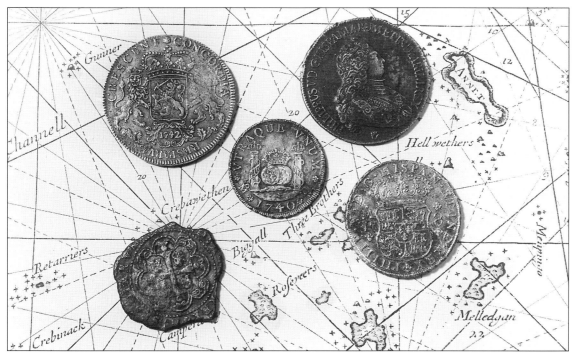

74. Coins recovered from the wreck of the *Hollandia* which sank off Scilly in 1743.

75. The sinking *Queen Mab* with other vessels in St Mary's harbour in 1872.

76. The *Association* which came to grief on Gilstone Rocks in 1707. The ship was the flagship of Admiral Sir Cloudesley Shovel.

77. The original tomb of Sir Cloudesley Shovel, Porthellick, St Mary's with the natural rock known as the Loaded Camel in the background. The Admiral lost his life when his flagship, the *Association* sank on the Gilstone Rock in 1707. He was later exhumed and re-interred in Westminster Abbey.

and drowned. The local Pilots' Widows' Fund was a well patronised charity. St Agnes pilots were always the busiest, being positioned closer to the main shipping lanes, and Jack Hicks who hailed from this island was the last pilot to retire in 1961. However, the heyday of piloting had ceased 100 years earlier with the coming of steampower.

Given that the Scilly archipelago is a maze of rocks, many of which are hidden at high water, it is not surprising that shipwrecks were common, especially before shipping had the advantage of modern day navigational aids. The seas of Scilly are a veritable graveyard for every type of vessel and over 200 wrecks were recorded in one period of 150 years. The rocks to the west of the islands are particularly treacherous, and the reefs which lie just below the surface have claimed thousands of lives as well as the vessels themselves.

It must be said that the Scillonians have always made valiant and heroic attempts to save the crews of these wrecks, with varying degrees of success. Their record of life-saving is well documented and records show that the rescuers were often lost. However, the foundering ships with their valuable cargoes have always proved to be a temptation to the islanders who gained them the reputation of 'wreckers'. The word in itself is misleading as it implies that islanders carried out deliberate acts of sabotage to the vessels for their own gain and that they were no better than pirates. This was far from the truth and wrecks were regarded as fair game. During the many years of poverty when the islanders turned to religion, shipwrecks were seen as gifts from the Almighty in an attempt to ease their economic hardship. This attitude was exemplified by a 12th-century charter associated with the Priory on Tresco, which stated that all wrecks should be 'enjoyed' by the monks.

One 18th-century clergyman included a request for wrecks in his prayers when in church he added: 'We pray thee hard, not that wrecks should happen, but if they do thou will guide them to the Scilly Isles for the benefit of the poor inhabitants'. Another parson in St Agnes' church mounted the pulpit and announced: 'Brethren, before I open the service, I have a sad duty to perform. There has been a wreck ...'. But before he could complete his statement, the church was empty. The next time he had a similar message for the congregation, he made sure that he was the first one to leave the church in the rush down to the beach!

When a shipwreck occurred a fleet of small boats and gigs was launched in Scilly to help the stricken vessel. After ensuring that the crew were safe, providing the ship had not gone under, the islanders would board the vessel and claim as much of the cargo as they had time to remove. In some cases, if the vessel was slow to sink, this would include the brass fittings, or anything else that was easily removable. Cargoes could be anything from liquors to flour to livestock, and the 'wreckers' were not particular so long as it was usable or had a market value.

The story of the Scilly shipwrecks could fill a book on its own, and it is probably only appropriate to mention two of the worst disasters. The first is the fleet of Admiral Sir Cloudesley Shovel, which came to grief on 22 October 1707, returning from the siege of Toulon. The Admiral's flagship, the HMS *Association,* broke up in minutes on the treacherous Gilstone Rock in the Western Rocks. The fireship *Firebrand* together with the 70-gun warship *Eagle* and the 50-gun *Romney,* also sank after striking rocks nearby.

Altogether 1,400 men, including Sir Cloudesley Shovel, were lost, there being only one survivor. The body of the admiral was washed up at Porth Hellick Bay, St Mary's, together with his sea chest and the stern board of his barge. His body was discovered by island women and he was interred in a shallow grave above the beach where he was washed ashore. Subsequently, Lady Shovel had his body exhumed and re-buried in Westminster Abbey with military honours.

The second major disaster was that of SS *Schiller* in May 1875. The vessel was one of the largest steamships of her day and was on passage from New York to Plymouth when she struck the Retarrier Ledges, again in the Western Rocks, and foundered. In some ways the incident has parallels with the *Titanic* in that a social function was in progress at the time of collision. Women passengers, dressed in their finery, began a mad scramble for the boats, but only two got safely away. A total of 311 crew and passengers lost their lives, and for a few days bodies were washed up all over the islands. A massive funeral took place on St Mary's and the bodies were conveyed to Old Town churchyard in 20 horse-drawn carts. Here they were buried in a mass grave which is now unmarked. One granite obelisk on the hillside survives to remind us of this terrible event.

During the 18th century some ship-building was taking place in the Islands, but only on a small scale to produce fishing vessels and small craft. However, during the Napoleonic Wars there was a growing demand for merchant vessels which coincided with the demise of the kelp industry, and

78.   The lifeboat of the fated SS *Schiller* on Town Beach, St Mary's in 1875.

79.   Filling in the SS *Schiller* graves in Old Town churchyard in 1875.

80. Old Town churchyard and the funeral procession for those drowned in the SS *Schiller* disaster in 1875.

81. One of many figureheads from wrecked vessels, on display at the Valhalla Museum, Tresco Gardens.

82.   The wreck of the *Torrey Canyon* on the Seven Stones in 1967. The ship was blown up to destroy its cargo
of oil which threatened the Scilly beaches.

83.   The *David Auterson*, the last of the barques to be built on Porthcressa in 1870.

84.   The *David Auterson* when complete on the Porthcressa ramps.

by 1835 a lucrative business had built up. In the heyday of the industry, between 1850 and 1870, there were no less than four shipyards operating on the tiny sandbar in Hugh Town. Two of these were situated on the Porthcressa bank and two on the opposite flank overlooking the harbour.

During the ship-building era, Hugh Town was a hive of activity with nearly everyone engaged in the industry. There were shipwrights, joiners and sailmakers working alongside coopers, riggers and rope makers. Above Town Beach were the timber yards where the wood was cut and treated before being used to build large hulks. The timber had to be imported and was delivered by special ships from the mainland.

In the early days ships were limited to 60 tons register by the old Navigation Acts. The tonnage restriction forced the islanders to build small

schooners and sloops, which soon gained a wide reputation throughout the world. By 1839, 20 of these small ships were registered. The restriction in size disappeared with the general boom in British shipping, and barques and brigantines of over 300 tons could then be manufactured.

By 1870 the islanders had moved into a period of prosperity and the ship-building industry was at its peak. However, the industrial revolution had produced vessels of iron and steel, powered by steam, and the days of timber ships were numbered. The last vessel built in the Porthcressa yards was the *David Auterson* in 1870, and the Town Beach yards went out of business with the launching of the *Gleaner* and *Rosevear* in 1878. There was a later burst of activity in the early 1880s but after that the shipyards were silent.

85. Shipbuilding on Town Beach in the 1870s.

86.   Shipbuilding on Town Beach, St Mary's, *c*.1865.

87.   Looking down the Strand, with the fishing fleet moored in the harbour.

88. An auction on Town
Quay in 1933 of a catch
confiscated from French
fishermen.

89.   The Mount's Bay fishing fleet in St Mary's harbour about 1900.

Chapter 7

Augustus Smith and Beyond

In 1831 the sixth Duke of Leeds. who had been connected to the Godolphin family by marriage, decided to terminate his lease on the Islands, and ownership reverted to the Crown. Many years of absentee landlords and the failure of the kelp industry had resulted in the Islands being on the brink of economic disaster. An indication of the state of Scilly was given by James Silk Buckingham, M.P. for Sheffield who visited the Islands at this time:

> Nothing could be conceived more primitive than the state of society, among which we were now thrown. The town of St Mary's had a Governor, two clergymen, three doctors, two lawyers and several merchants who were all smuggling; the rest were mere tradesmen, shopkeepers and boatmen, who lived partly by fishing, still more by smuggling, and worst of all, it was said, by visiting wrecked vessels and helping themselves freely to whatever could be saved from destruction.

Buckingham mentions all the maritime activities that have previously been discussed, with the exception of shipbuilding which was yet to come. The commencement of shipbuilding coincided with the start of a new and prosperous era, following the renewal of the lease in November 1834 to a Mr. Smith, who was to become the new Lord Proprietor. Augustus John Smith was a gentlemen from Berkhamsted, Herts, who had been educated at Harrow and Oxford. One of his desires had been to 'improve the lot of the working classes', for which he received little support on the mainland.

His arrival in Scilly in February 1835 was a godsend to the islanders, although at first his harsh rule caused resentment. Many saw him as a rich outsider interfering with their daily routine, but his very appearance demanded respect and his word soon became law. On his arrival he took up residence on St Mary's in the house of the Stewards of the Duke of Leeds, but soon he was to break with tradition and build himself a house on the island of Tresco close by the ruins of the Priory which later became known as Tresco Abbey after the early foundation.

After many tours of inspection he realised that there was no basis for economic farming in the Islands, and that his tenants owned scattered pieces of land because of sub-divisions which occurred whenever a farmer died and left a land-holding to his children. Augustus started from square one: he

90. Augustus Smith, proprietor of the Islands from 1835 to 1872.

91.   Tresco Abbey, built in 1836 as a home for Augustus Smith.

92.   Ruined cottages on South Hill, Samson, dating from the evacuation of the island in 1855.

93.   A group of geology students in 1890 at Armorel's Cottage, Samson, which is said to have inspired
Sir Walter Besant when he wrote the novel, *Armorel of Lyonesse*.

re-allocated land to form workable economic farming units and introduced a system of inheritance
whereby land was passed to the eldest son, all other
offspring being forced to find other employment.

Smith was also responsible for the depopula-
tion of the island of Samson in 1855 when he
evicted the last families there for their own good.
Resettlement on Samson had taken place around
1683 and the story goes that in the 18th century the
island was a penal colony for undesirables, and that
the Webber and Woodcock families formed the
basis of a new settlement. They were ordered to
leave their homes on St Mary's by the Court of
Twelve. Gradually the numbers grew until the
population was around fifty. These were reduced
during the Napoleonic Wars when a ship carrying
19 Samson men hit the Wolf Rock and sank with
the loss of all hands. The lack of man-power on the
island resulted in the community fighting a losing
battle against the environment. Five families were
deported across the water to St Mary's. The remains of their cottages together with a dried-up
spring can still be seen on the south hill at Samson.

Augustus then turned to the problem of surplus
population and unemployment. He found jobs in an
improvement scheme which included the building

of roads and miles of granite boundary walls on St
Mary's and Tresco. A more vigorous job was the
blasting of sea-bed rock between Tresco and Bryher
to widen the New Grimsby Channel. On Tresco
itself there was the actual building of his own house
and the eventual clearance of a hillside on which
his famous botanical gardens were planted. On St
Mary's he provided a new parish church in Hugh
Town, for which he laid the foundation stone in
October 1836. The building was finished in August
1838 and consecrated by the Bishop of Exeter. The
other important achievement of 1838 was the
extension of the Old Quay, built in 1601, as far as
Rat Island. This pier was again extended in 1889.

Augustus Smith is probably best remembered
for his reforms in the field of education. He built
new schools on the Islands and advocated that
education should be compulsory some thirty years
before the Foster Act ruled to this effect on the
mainland. He ensured that the schools were well
attended by charging a penny a week for each pupil
if they attended and two pence a week if they
played truant. Augustus himself took night classes
on the art of navigation. As a result, many boats
built in Scilly at this time were manned by Scillonian
seamen, some fitted for the rôle of officers.

94.   Augustus Smith holding a picnic on Tresco, *c.*1850.

In July 1872 Augustus Smith died in a Plymouth hotel, four days after he had designed his own memorial which stands on Abbey Hill, Tresco. During his reign in Scilly he had dramatically improved the lives of the Scillonians, their land, houses and sanitation. He had suppressed smuggling, and introduced a post office service and compulsory fire insurance. When he died, the islanders were enjoying a period of prosperity and full employment.

Augustus was succeeded by his nephew Lieutenant Thomas Algernon Dorrien-Smith who carried on his uncle's good work. He initially set about creating a more fitting memorial for Augustus in the form of St Nicholas' church on Tresco, which was completed in 1879 and consecrated in 1882 by the Bishop of Truro. Other churches on the off-islands were rebuilt at this time with the usual Victorian restoration. All Saints', Bryher was originally built in 1742 in a cruciform pattern with a sturdy west tower. In contrast the church on St Agnes, which dates from 1821, is an unpretentious building with a fine stained glass window.

St Martin's church, on the island of that name, is perhaps of more interest and is believed to have been built on the site of an 11th-/12th-century chapel and graveyard. The present building was erected in 1683 by the Godolphin Steward, and repaired by the Rev. George Woodley in 1821. After being struck by lightning in 1866, it was rebuilt by Augustus Smith. A block of granite built into the east wall is believed to be a medieval cross base, whilst a pillar in the churchyard is the base of an ancient sundial.

The dangers of navigation in Scilly eventually led to the erection of lighthouses. The first was built on St Agnes by Trinity House in 1680. The first light was a coal fire lit in an iron brazier inside a lantern, which was replaced in 1790 by oil lamps. The original brazier can still be seen as an ornament in Tresco Gardens. The lighthouse was superseded by a steel one on Peninnis Head, St Mary's, in 1911, but is still a prominent daymark for shipping. A granite daymark on Chapel Down, St Martin's, painted red and white, was erected by Thomas Ekin in 1683. The date stone has been wrongly inscribed and reads 1637.

In the north of the islands a circular lighthouse was built on the three acres of Round Island in 1887, and shows a flashing red light; but perhaps the best known of the stone sentinels is Bishop Rock, which is situated in the treacherous waters amongst the Western Rocks. Trinity House were under pressure from mariners to provide this granite

95.   The school on St Martin's island.

96.   The Prince of Wales, later King Edward VII, with Lieutenant T. A. Dorrien-Smith returning from Star Castle in 1902.

97. St Nicholas' church, Tresco, completed in 1879 as a memorial to Augustus Smith, governor of the Islands.

98. St Martin's church, built around 1683 by Thomas Ekin, the Godolphin Steward. The church was rebuilt by George Woodley in 1820 and repaired by Augustus Smith in 1866 after being struck by lightning.

tower which rises to 167 feet. However, the first attempt in 1847 was an open iron structure of 120 feet high, which was washed away by heavy seas in February 1850, even before it came into use. It was soon realised that a much more sturdy structure of solid granite would be needed to survive the power of the sea, whose waves have been known to reach the top of the tower.

The neighbouring island of Rosevear was used as a base, and during the construction the workforce lived

in 1976, and now the lighthouse is fully automated.

As one might imagine, the Scillonian lifeboat service is one of the busiest in the British Isles, and many of the crew members have been decorated for their acts of bravery. Prior to 1837, lifesaving and salvage work were carried out by pilot boats and gigs, but in that year a site on St Mary's was provided for the first lifeboat house. The original lifeboat was transferred from

99. Troy Town Maze, Castella Down, St Agnes, believed to have been laid out in 1729 by the bored son of a lighthouse keeper, but possibly with more ancient origins. There are recent copies elsewhere in Scilly.

there alongside all their building materials. Lighthouse builder Mr. N. Douglas was selected to supervise its construction and work started in 1851. Its erection was a major engineering feat, involving incredibly hard work, which is indicated by the fact that it took a whole year to lay the base. Even when it was completed in 1858 the whole building vibrated when hit by the Atlantic breakers. The tower was strengthened in 1874 and again in the 1880s with final completion in 1887. Light was provided by oil lamp until electricity was installed in 1973. The lighthouse was manned by keepers who were often stranded there for months in bad weather. However, a helicopter pad was added

Brighton and was in use until 1855 when it sunk. From 1855 until 1874 there was no boat on the Islands until the *Henry Dundas* was launched. In 1890 a further lifeboat house was built at Periglis, St Agnes, which was in use until 1920. During its lifetime the *James* and *Caroline* and two versions of the *Charles Deere James* were launched innumerable times and saved many lives.

Regular boats linking the islands with Penzance in Cornwall probably started in the 1850s with the cutter *Ariadne*, which was replaced in 1858 by the steamboat *Scotia*. In the following year the *Little Western* also came into service and

100. St Agnes' Lighthouse erected by Trinity House in 1680. It now acts as a daymark and an observatory.

was skippered by Captain Frank Tregarthen, who insisted that passengers should stay at his St Mary's hotel, which today carries his name. In 1872 the *Little Western* and the auxiliary vessel *Earl of Arran* were both wrecked. The paddle steamers *Guide* and *Queen of the Bay* kept the service going until 1875 when the Lady of the Isles took up the run. Then followed the *Lyonesse* in 1888.

In 1919 the Isles of Scilly Steamship Company was formed and ran the *Lapwing* and the *Peninnis* until 1926 when the first *Scillonian* was launched. This, like all the previous vessels, was used mainly to transport goods to the Islands and deliver to the mainland. By 1956 when the Islands had been discovered by holiday-makers, the Company realised that they needed a larger boat with accommodation for passengers and cargo, and the larger *Scillonian II* came into service. In 1965 it was joined by the *Queen of the Isles* and both were replaced by the present *Scillonian III*, launched in 1977. The journey from Penzance to Scilly is normally a rough one, mainly because the Scillonian boats are equipped with a flat bottom as St Mary's harbour is comparatively shallow.

101.   The Daymark, Chapel Down, St Martin's, erected by Thomas Ekin in 1683. To the right are the ruins of a signal station in use during the Napoleonic Wars. This went out of use in 1810.

102.   Visitors to Round Island Lighthouse in 1890.

103. The first Bishop Rock Lighthouse that was washed away in 1850.

104. Recasing the Bishop Rock Lighthouse.

105. Houses on the small western isle of Rosevear, built to house the workforce constructing Bishop Rock Lighthouse.

106.   Bishop Rock Lighthouse at sunset.

107. Inside the Bishop Rock Lighthouse, *c*.1930.

108. A lighthouse keeper loads detonators on Bishop Rock Lighthouse.

109.   Looking down from the lighthouse at a rough swell.

110. Relieving the Bishops
      Rock Lighthouse by boat.

111. Lifeboat Slip, Periglis, St Agnes which was in use from 1890-1920. The *Charles Deere James* lifeboat
      was in service between 1911 and 1918.

112. The launching of the lifeboat *Cunard*. The actress Flora Robson, who has family on St Mary's, is
shaking hands with coxswain Matt Lethbridge senior.

113. The *Earl of Arran*, a passenger boat which foundered on Nornour in 1872.

114. Passengers aboard the *Lady of the Isles* in 1896.

115.   The *Lyonesse*, a steamship serving the Islands from 1888.

116.   The *Scillonian* (1926-56) aground on Wingletang, St Agnes in 1951.

RMV SCILLONIAN

LAURENCE DUNN

117.   The RMV *Scillonian II* which came into service in 1956.

118.   The *Scillonian III* loading from supply boats at St Mary's Quay.

119. William Trevellick and family at Rocky Hill Farm greenhouse. The blooms are 'Grand Monarques'.

120.   Three ladies from the Watts family travelling on The Parade, Hugh Town.

The improvement in communications during the 19th century was to prove an advantage to a new industry which virtually replaced ship-building in the Islands. For centuries the Scillonians had relied on the sea for their living, and had failed to recognise the potential of the frost-free climate that they enjoyed and the possibility of exploiting the land for commercial agriculture. It was around 1873 that the Victorians started a fashion for buying cut flowers, and it was this move that eventually spurred William Trevellick of Rocky Hill, St Mary's into sending a hatbox of blooms to the Covent Garden market in 1879 for which he received the sum of seven shillings and sixpence.

The permanent establishment of the industry, which continues today, was mainly due to T. A. Dorrien-Smith who travelled to Holland to study the cultivation of bulbs and returned in 1882 with 190 varieties. He encouraged the islanders to turn their smallholdings into flower farms and to surround the bulb fields with windbreaks. The main varieties grown were daffodils and narcissi and the first of these bloomed in early December, enabling the islanders to market their product in advance of their competitors. By 1885 they were exporting 65 tons of flowers which rose to a peak of 1,200. It is said that the Scillonians produced up to 60 million blooms in the good years.

From this time onwards the islanders never again knew poverty. The prosperity of Scilly is reflected in the growth of Hugh Town from the Garrison with its parish church, new streets, housing and public buildings. The original settlement was mainly huddled at the western end of the isthmus below Star Castle. The erection of a town hall in 1889 heralded the arrival of democracy in the Islands, with the formation of the Isles of Scilly Council to work hand-in-hand with the Duchy of Cornwall. Each off-island has representatives on this Council who generally administer the day-to-day running of Scilly.

Like all communities, Scilly was affected by the two World Wars, although the Islands suffered very little from bombardment. Its strategic position on the map ensured a military occupation and additional fortifications were added. During the Great War Tresco became the headquarters for a seaplane base which took action against enemy U-boats, and St Mary's had a naval sub-base. A similar situation existed in Second World War with many islanders seeing action in the Merchant Navy.

121. Ladies gathering daffodils for the London market.

122. William Trevellick, the father of the flower industry in Scilly, at Rocky Hill Farm, St Mary's.

123.   Bulb fields being ploughed on St Martin's in the early days of the flower industry.

124.   Home-made wooden flower boxes being loaded on board the *Lyonesse*, *c*.1910.

125.   Cardboard cartons for flowers arriving at St Martin's.

Today the mainstay of the economy of Scilly is tourism which, when it started, was complementary to the flower industry. The improvement in communications made it possible to travel to the Islands for an annual break and it was not long before the climate and natural beauty attracted visitors on a regular basis. New hotels were built and these were supplemented with guest houses to cater for all classes of tourist. The introduction of an air service and the building of an airport on St Mary's in 1937 made access easier, and visitors travelled on eight-seater Dragon Rapides, until a helicopter service was intro-

duced in 1964. The St Mary's heliport has now been extended to take larger fixed-wing aeroplanes and another heliport opened on Tresco.

The Isles of Scilly today remain largely unspoilt by the requirements of modern life. On the off-islands there are quiet places where little has changed since the first settlers landed in prehistoric times and it is possible to sit and contemplate those early days of the Islands' history. Relics of these former days are to be seen everywhere and are protected by the authorities. The Islands are unique and will always remain so.

126. St Mary's parish church, Hugh Town, built by Augustus Smith in 1838. The planks on the left have been sawn for shipbuilding. This photograph dates from 1870.

127.   The Bank, Hugh Town, St Mary's, c.1870.

128.   The Parade, Park and Town Hall, built in 1889, Hugh Town taken earlier this century.

129.   The anti-U-boat seaplane base on Tresco during the First World War.

130.   The administrative centre on Tresco, converted from the seaplane base.

131. The carpet cart visits the Islands at the turn of the century.

132.   Hugh Town in the Great Blizzard of 1891, one of the rare occasions when snow fell in Scilly.

133.   A De Havilland Dragon Rapide; the aircraft that was used when St Mary's airport opened in 1937.

134.   A seaplane in the harbour at St Mary's. At the back of Town Beach is the *Holgates Hotel*, which was pulled down in 1977.

135.   Sir Alan Cobham lands on the golf course, St Mary's in the 1920s.

136. John Tregear, a Scillonian character, below
Buzza Hill, *c*.1868.

137. Horatio Nelson, the one-man police force in
Scilly from 1865 to 1875.

138. The Prince of Wales, later Edward VIII, at Pelistry, St Mary's, with Tom Tregear in 1933.

139. Sir Harold Wilson holding a press conference on Samson when he was Prime Minister in 1965. Lord Wilson has a cottage on St Mary's.

140.   May Day in Hugh Town, 1876.

141.   Early visitors amongst the Western Rocks in Victorian times.

The following selection of photographs depicts Hugh Town past and Hugh Town present:

142.   Church Street and The Parade, Hugh Town, *c.*1887.

143.   The same scene in 1992, showing the addition of the Town Hall and Park.

144.   Church Street, Hugh Town, *c.*1890-1900. The scene shows the children from the Infant School on the left which was built in 1854.

145.   The same scene in 1992. The Infant School is now the Church Hall, and the Isles of Scilly Museum, opened in 1967, occupies the neighbouring building.

146.   Hugh Street, Hugh Town, *c.*1910, looking towards the Garrison.

147.   Hugh Street in 1992, with modern buildings on the left and several shops.

148.   Hugh Street looking towards the Town Hall, *c.*1900.

149.   The same scene in 1992.

150. Porthcressa Beach and Hugh Town from Buzza Hill, *c*.1900.

151. Porthcressa Beach and Hugh Town today, showing the increase in housing.

Bibliography

Arlott, John, *Island Camera* (1972).

Ashbee, Paul, *Ancient Scilly* (1974).

Borlase, William, *Observation on the Ancient and Present State of the Islands in Scilly* (1756).

Bowley, R. L., *The Fortunate Islands* (1980).

Cornwall Archaeological Unit, *Scilly's Archaeological Heritage* (1992).

Heath, Robert, *A Natural and Historical Account of the Islands of Scilly* (1750).

Mumford, Clive, *Portrait of the Isles of Scilly* (1967).

Over, Luke, *The Kelp Industry in Scilly* (1987).

Over, Luke, *Visitors Guide to the Archaeology of Scilly* (1974).

Thomas, Charles, *Exploration of a Drowned Landscape* (1985).

Troutbeck, John, *A Survey of the Ancient and Present State of the Scilly Islands* (1796).

Woodley, George, *A View of the Present State of the Scilly Islands* (1822).

Index